RECORD BREAKERS

RECORD-BREAKING CARS

DANIEL GILPIN

PowerKiDS press
New York

J629.222
GIL

Published in 2012 by The Rosen Publishing Group Inc.
29 East 21st Street, New York, NY 10010

First Edition

Senior Editor: Debbie Foy
Designer: Rob Walster
Picture Researcher: Kate Lockley

Library of Congress Cataloging-in-Publication Data

Gilpin, Daniel.
Record-breaking cars / by Daniel Gilpin. -- 1st ed.
   p. cm. -- (Record breakers)
Includes index.
ISBN 978-1-4488-5289-5 (library binding)
1. Automobiles--Juvenile literature. 2. World records--Juvenile
literature. I. Title.
TL147.G5474 2012
629.222--dc22

2010047272

Manufactured in China
CPSIA Compliance Information: Batch # WAS1102PK: For Further Information
contact Rosen Publishing, New York, New York at 1-800-237-9932

Abbreviations used:

ft. = feet
m = meters
in. = inches
cm = centimeters
lb. = pounds
kg = kilograms
km = kilometers
mm = millimeters
mph = miles per hour
km/h = kilometers per hour
hp = horsepower

Tricky words are listed in "But What
Does That Mean?" on page 31.

WHAT'S INSIDE?

APPLE $19.00

BUGATTI VEYRON

The Bugatti Veyron speeds up faster than any other car on the road. In a race from 0–60 miles (0–97 km) per hour, it would leave the world's fastest road car behind!

FASTEST ACCELERATION!

Can You Believe It?

The Bugatti Veyron is a four-wheel drive, just like the Land Rover. This is unusual for sports cars because most are two-wheel drive.

The Veyron's engine is more powerful than most Formula One racing cars!

WOW!

TOP SPEED: 253 MPH (317 KM/H)
0–60 MPH (0–97 KM/H): 2.4 SECONDS
MAX POWER OUTPUT: 1,001 HP
ENGINE: 8 LITER W16
PRICE (NEW): $1,456,000

The Bugatti Veyron's interior is designed for comfort and luxury.

HUMMER H1 ALPHA WAGON

The H1 Alpha Wagon is the world's largest production car. It was adapted from the Humvee military vehicle, which was designed for off-road operations and is used by the U.S. Army.

Can You Believe It?

The H1 Alpha Wagon does just 12 miles (19 km) per gallon. Hummer stopped making it in 2006, when new laws in the U.S. made such low levels illegal.

There are also convertible and pickup versions of the H1 Alpha Wagon.

The Alpha Wagon clears the ground by a huge 16 in. (40 cm)!

WOW!

LENGTH: 15 FT. 4 IN. (4.67 M)
WIDTH: 7 FT. 2 IN. (2.18 M)
WEIGHT: 8,114 LB. (3,684 KG)
TOP SPEED: 90 MPH (145 KM/H)
ENGINE: 6.6 LITER V8 TURBODIESEL

NUNA 2

Nuna 2 is the world's fastest solar-powered car. Using nothing but the energy from sunlight, it can reach speeds of more than 100 miles (160 km) per hour!

Can You Believe It?

To reach 60 miles (100 km) per hour, Nuna 2 needs just 1,650 watts of electricity. This is the same amount of power that is used by a hair dryer!

The "pilot" needs to be in a lying down position to drive Nuna 2.

WOW!

TOP SPEED: 105 MPH (169 KM/H)
LENGTH: 16 FT. 5 IN. (5 M)
WIDTH: 5 FT. 11 IN. (1.8 M)
NUMBER OF SOLAR CELLS: 3,000
COST TO BUILD: $488,000

Nuna 2 gathers energy from
the sun by using solar cells
that cover its whole surface.

PAGANI ZONDA TRICOLORE

This amazing car costs more to buy new than any other car ever made!

Can You Believe It?

Only one Pagani Zonda Tricolore was ever made! It was built in 2010 to celebrate the 50th anniversary of the Italian Red Arrows.

Before the Zonda Tricolore was built, the record was held for 12 years by the Mercedes Benz CLK/LM.

WOW!

TOP SPEED: 217 MPH (349 KM/H)
0–60 MPH (0–97 KM/H): 3.4 SECONDS
MAX POWER OUTPUT: 678 HP
ENGINE: 7.3 LITER V12
PRICE (NEW): $2,144,000

On the Other Hand...

With only one ever made, the Zonda Tricolore is also the world's rarest supercar!

Built in India, the Tata Nano is the world's cheapest production car. When it first went on sale in 2009, it cost just 123,000 rupees ($2,584).

THRUST SSC

FASTEST CAR EVER!

Thrust SSC is the fastest car on Earth! On October 13, 1997, it became the first car to go faster than the speed of sound. And two days later, this amazing car set a new land speed record!

Can You Believe It?

Thrust SSC has the same engine power as 145 Formula One racing cars—or 1,000 Ford Escorts!

Thrust SSC during its record-breaking run. It was driven here by a Royal Air Force pilot.

CONTENDERS

The Thrust SSC team are now developing another jet-powered car. It is called Bloodhound SSC and is designed to travel at more than 1,000 miles (1,600 km) per hour!

Thrust SSC's engines were developed for jet fighter planes.

WOW!

TOP SPEED: 763 MPH (317 KM/H)
MAX POWER OUTPUT: 110,000 HP
LENGTH: 54 FT. (16.5 M)
WEIGHT: 23,153 LB. (10,500 KG)
ENGINES: TWO ROLLS ROYCE
SPEY 205 JET ENGINES

13

TOYOTA COROLLA

BEST-SELLING!

The Toyota Corolla is the world's best-selling car. Since it was first made in 1966, 35 million of them have been sold!

Can You Believe It?

On average, there has been one new Toyota Corolla sold every 40 seconds, for the past 40 years!

WOW!

NUMBER SOLD: 35 MILLION
COUNTRIES PRODUCING: 15
TOP SPEED: 131 MPH (211 KM/H)
0–60 MPH (0–97 KM/H): 7.8 SECONDS
NAME IN THE UK: TOYOTA AURIS

BUGATTI "ROYALE" TYPE 41

The Bugatti "Royale" Type 41 was designed and built to transport royalty. Only six of these huge cars were ever made!

Can You Believe It?

This car cost much more second-hand than any new car ever did.
In 1990, a used Bugatti "Royale" sold for $15 million!

MOST EXPENSIVE EVER!

WOW!

NUMBER BUILT: 6
YEARS MADE: 1929–1933
LENGTH: 21 FT. (6.4 M)
WEIGHT: 7,001 LB. (3,175 KG)
PRICE NEW (IN 1930): $14,640

ULTIMATE AERO TT

FASTEST ROAD CAR!

The Ultimate Aero is the world's fastest production car. The record-breaking TT (Twin Turbo) version came out in 2007, and can reach an incredible 256 miles (412 km) per hour!

Can You Believe It?

There are plans to build an electric version (or EV) of the Ultimate Aero. This will challenge the record for the world's fastest electric car. The EV is expected to reach speeds of 208 miles (335 km) per hour!

The speed record was set on the Shelby SuperCars test track in the United States.

The Ultimate Aero TT has amazing "butterfly wing" doors!

WOW!

TOP SPEED: 256 MPH (412 KM/H)
0–60 MPH (0–97 KM/H): 2.8 SECONDS
MAX POWER OUTPUT: 1,287 HP
ENGINE: 6.3 LITER V8 TWIN TURBO
PRICE (NEW): $536,000

VW L1

The VW L1 is the world's most fuel-efficient car. It has a small diesel engine combined with an electric motor. Its streamlined body keeps fuel use down.

Can You Believe It?

The VW L1 is more than just a concept car. It should be on our roads by 2013!

On the Other Hand...

The world's least fuel-efficient road car is the Lamborghini Murcielago. In city traffic, it does an average of 8 miles (12 km) per gallon.

MICHELIN

WOW!

MILES PER GALLON: 189
TOP SPEED: 99 MPH (159 KM/H)
0–60 MPH (0–97 KM/H):
14.3 SECONDS
MAX POWER OUTPUT: 29 HP
ENGINE: 0.8 LITER
TURBODIESEL HYBRID

The VW L1 is designed to carry two people, one behind the other.

The sleek VW L1 weighs just 840 lb. (380 kg)!

DODGE VIPER SRT-10

The Dodge Viper SRT-10 has the biggest engine of any production car. Its engine is so loud that you can hear a Dodge Viper coming a long time before you can see it!

Can You Believe It?

The Viper's engine was based on the Chrysler LA, which is an engine used in American trucks.

The 10-cylinder Viper engine has powerful twin turbos.

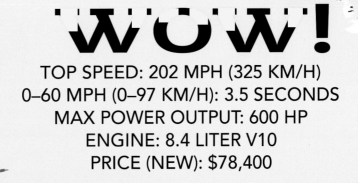

WOW!

TOP SPEED: 202 MPH (325 KM/H)
0–60 MPH (0–97 KM/H): 3.5 SECONDS
MAX POWER OUTPUT: 600 HP
ENGINE: 8.4 LITER V10
PRICE (NEW): $78,400

CONTENDERS

The engine of the Ultimate Aero TT is smaller than the Viper's, but it is much more powerful. It produces an amazing 1,287 hp!

MORGAN 4/4

The Morgan 4/4 was first built in 1936. New cars are still being made at the original factory site, in the heart of the English countryside.

Can You Believe It?

The 4/4 was the first four-wheeled car built by Morgan. Before 1936, the Morgan company only built three-wheelers!

OLDEST STILL MADE!

"4/4" stands for 4 wheels and 4 cylinders!

WOW!

TOP SPEED: 115 MPH (185 KM/H)
0–60 MPH (0–97 KM/H):
8 SECONDS
ENGINE: 1.8 LITER 4-CYLINDER
PRICE IN 1936: $310
PRICE TODAY: $43,200

With the top down, you can see the 4/4's fine leather interior.

CONTENDERS

The design of the original VW Beetle was unchanged from 1938 until 2003. The last VW Beetles to be sold were built in Mexico.

INSPIRATION

Inspiration is the world's fastest steam-powered car. On August 27, 2009, a new world record was set on a desert track in California.

Can You Believe It?

The British-made Inspiration broke the world record held since 1906 by the American Stanley Steamer. At that time, the Stanley Steamer was the fastest land vehicle on Earth. It was also the first land vehicle ever to travel at more than 124 miles (200 km) per hour.

The UK Inspiration team, with their record-breaking car.

WOW!

TOP SPEED: 151 MPH (243 KM/H)
MAX POWER OUTPUT: 360 HP
LENGTH: 25 FT. 2 IN. (7.66 M)
WIDTH: 5 FT. 7 IN. (1.7 M)
WEIGHT: 6,720 LB. (3,051 KG)

Inspiration is put
through its paces in the
Californian desert.

PEEL P50

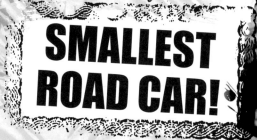

The Peel P50 is the world's smallest production car. It was only built during 1963–64, and its tiny engine was first designed to power mopeds.

Can You Believe It?

The P50 has no reverse gear. To turn the car around, the driver gets out and lifts the car up using a handle on the back!

WOW!

LENGTH: 4 FT. 5 IN. (1.34 M)
WIDTH: 3 FT. 3 IN. (0.99 M)
WEIGHT: 130 LB. (59 KG)
TOP SPEED: 38 MPH (61 KM/H)
ENGINE: 0.05 LITER,
TWO-STROKE

The P50 was built on the Isle of Man—where there is no speed limit!

The former world's smallest man sits in the world's smallest production car.

CONTENDERS

Some one-of-a-kind, homemade cars are even smaller than the P50. Perhaps the smallest is Wind-up, built by car fanatic Perry Watkins. It is less that half the size of the P50!

LAMBORGHINI GALLARDO

The Lamborghini Gallardo is one of the world's fastest and most expensive cars. Two of them zoom around on the streets of Rome, Italy, as police cars!

Can You Believe It?

Each of Rome's police Gallardos are equipped with a small refrigerator! They are used to carry human organs needed for transplant operations.

Rome's police Gallardos are fully equipped with radios and speed detectors.

CONTENDERS

Other countries also have super-fast police cars. In Germany, the fastest is a Brabus CLS V12, nicknamed The Rocket. In Austria, some police officers drive the Porsche 911.

WOW!

TOP SPEED: 197 MPH (317 KM/H)
0–60 MPH (0–97 KM/H): 4.1 SECONDS
MAX POWER OUTPUT: 552 HP
ENGINE: 5.2 LITER V10
PRICE (NEW): $224,480

TEST YOURSELF!

Can you remember facts about the record-breaking cars in this book? Test yourself here by answering these questions!

1. Which car is bigger, a Peel P50 or a Hummer H1 Alpha Wagon?
2. Which Italian city has Lamborghini police cars?
3. What car made $15 million when it was sold in 1990?
4. In which year did Thrust SSC set the world land speed record?
5. How many Corollas have been sold throughout the world?
6. When was the Pagani Zonda Tricolore built?
7. Which is quicker from 0–60 mph (0–97 km/h), the Ultimate Aero TT or the Bugatti Veyron?
8. In which country is the Morgan 4/4 made?
9. Was the Stanley Steamer an American or a British car?
10. Which country was the last one to make new VW Beetles?

Answers

1. A Hummer H1 Alpha Wagon
2. Rome
3. A Bugatti "Royale" Type 41
4. 1997
5. 35 million
6. 2010
7. The Bugatti Veyron
8. England, UK
9. An American car
10. Mexico

BUT WHAT DOES THAT MEAN?

acceleration   How fast a car speeds up.

concept car   A one-of-a-kind car, built to test an idea, but usually not for sale.

convertible   A car with a foldaway roof.

cylinders   The parts of a car's engine where the fuel is lit, and turned into energy and carried to the wheels.

fanatic   A person who is devoted to an activity or hobby.

hp   The power of a car's engine is measured in horsepower. The higher the horsepower of an engine, the more powerful it is.

hybrid   A car that uses a combination of gas (or diesel) and electric power.

illegal   This means against the law.

interior   The inside of a car.

liter   A measurement of volume. The size of a car's engine (the total volume of its cylinders) is measured in liters.

max power output   The maximum amount of power that a car's engine can make and carry to the wheels.

off-road   Cars that are built to travel off public roads and over rough ground.

pickup   A truck with an open back.

production car   A car made in a factory and sold for use on the road.

reverse gear   The gear on a car that allows it to go backward.

solar car   A car powered by electricity, made by solar cells on its bodywork.

solar cell   A tiny device used for turning the energy from sunlight into electricity.

speed of sound   The speed that sound travels through the air, which is 761 miles (1,225 km) per hour!

streamlined   A vehicle with a smooth shape, which allows air to flow freely over it and so travel faster!

transplant   To implant an organ into another person's body.

used   Another word for second-hand.

v10   An engine with 10 cylinders arranged in a V shape. A V12 engine has 12 cylinders arranged in a V shape.

w16   An engine with 16 cylinders arranged in a W shape.

FURTHER INFORMATION, WEB SITES, AND INDEX

Places to go

Indianapolis Motor Speedway Hall of Fame Museum, Indianapolis, Indiana
The top museum devoted to auto racing features many Indianapolis 500-winning vehicles and more.

National Automobile Museum, Reno, Nevada
Exhibits feature vehicles from every era, including classics and one-of-a-kind cars.

Black Rock Desert, Nevada
This is where the Thrust CC land speed record attempt took place in 1997.

Books to read

Exotic Cars
by John Lamm (Motorbooks, 2008)

Guinness World Records, 2011
(Guinness World Records, 2010)

Super Cars
by Denny Von Finn (Bellwether Media, 2009)

Web Sites

Due to the changing nature of Internet links, PowerKids Press has developed an online list of Web sites related to the subject of this book. This site is updated regularly. Please use this link to access this list:
http://www.powerkidslinks.com/record/cars/

Index